Hawthorden

𝔅𝔩𝔞𝔠𝔨 𝔄𝔤𝔫𝔢𝔰,

OR THE

DEFENCE OF DUNBAR

BY AGNES, COUNTESS OF MARCH,

IN THE YEAR 1338

———

LONDON·

PRINTED FOR F. C. AND J. RIVINGTON,
62, ST PAUL'S CHURCH-YARD,
By Bye and Law, St. John's Square, Clerkenwell

———

1804.

ADVERTISEMENT.

THESE Verses may serve to bring forward a splendid portion of British History, at a time when instances of loyalty, patriotism, and successful valour may be useful. They may serve also to inspire a love for the union of the three kingdoms, and a proper confidence in the strength and spirit of the country to resist a French invasion—topics which should be insisted on in every shape, which may catch the attention or arrest the imagination.

November, 1803

AN

ACCOUNT

OF THE

SIEGE OF DUNBAR.

1338.

IT is pleasant to reflect that our Countrymen of
North Britain have never been subdued by an in-
vading enemy, even the proud waves of the Roman
Empire wasted their strength in vain against the
mountains of Caledonia Scotland has sometimes

been ravaged, but cannot be said to have been subdued. It suffered little comparatively from the incursions of the Northern nations, and nothing from the Normans. The homage exacted by Henry the Second after the battle of Alnwick was but a feudal ceremony, and was soon dispensed with. The inroads of Edward the First were but so much blood spilt on the ground, their traces were soon worn out. Our English Hero, Edward the Third, marched his victorious armies *four* times through the heart of Scotland, yet what was the reward of his labours? No sooner did he withdraw his troops than the spirit of ancient Caledonia revived, and the people seemed to have forgotten that he had ever invaded them. The English Faction however was so strong at the time, that David Bruce was forced to retire to France during his minority. Among

the brave Supporters of their rightful Sovereign *.
his low estate, we may reckon the Countess of
March, the daughter of Thomas Randal, Earl of
Murray, and nephew of Robert Bruce. This won-
derful Lady who was commonly called *black* Agnes,
and is known in history by that name, gallantly
defended Dunbar, in the absence of her husband,
during a grievous siege of nineteen weeks, in the
conclusion of the year 1337 and the beginning of
the year following The besiegers were part of the
victorious army which Edward the Third had left
behind him after his *fourth* and last invasion,
headed by the Earls of Salisbury and Arundel,
brave men and confummate generals. We may
judge of the esteem in which they were held in
that gallant age from the circumstance that the
Earl of Arundel was soon afterwards Constable at

the battle of Crecy, and with the Earl of South-
ampton led on the second division; and that at
the battle of Poictiers the Earl of Salisbury with
the Earl of Suffolk commanded the rear. One
may consider them therefore as knights companions to the *black* Prince. One helped him to
win the crest of feathers, the other assisted him
when by his modesty as well as his heroism he
covered it with glory, bringing the king of France
himself a prisoner to London.

Though Dunbar was assailed by such a gallant
army and such able generals, the Countess of March
only laughed at their vain attempt, standing on
the walls whenever there happened to be a truce,
and throwing out taunting reflections on her ad-
versaries, in order to keep up the spirits of her

men. She performed all the duties of a bold and vigilant commander, animating the garrison by her exhortations, munificence and example. When the battering engines of the besiegers hurled stones against the battlements, she, as in scorn, ordered one of her female attendants to wipe off the dirt with her handkerchief And one day when the Earl of Salisbury commanded that enormous warlike machine called the Sow, which he had formed with great labour, to be advanced to the foot of the walls, she scoffingly advised him to take good care of his Sow, for she would soon make her cast her pigs (meaning the men within it) and then ordered melted pitch and burning sulphur and the like, with huge stones and beams to be let fall on it, by which she destroyed it and the poor little

pigs, as ⸱ Major calls them, which were lurking
under it

The Earl of Salisbury finding so stout a re-
sistance attempted to gain the Castle by treachery,
and accordingly bribed the Porter, and those who
had the charge of the gate, promising them a great
‑eward if they would leave it open. This they
agreed to do, but disclosed the whole transaction
to the Countess

Salisbury himself commanded the party who
were to enter, and according to agreement found
the gate open, and was advancing at the head of
ᴸus men, when John Copeland, one of his at

⸱ John Major, Lib. 5. c. 15

tendants, hastily passing before him, the Portcullis was let down, and Copeland mistaken for his Lord, remained a prisoner. Agnes, who from a high tower was observing the event, cried out to Salisbury jeeringly, " Farewell, Montague, I in- " tended that you should have supped with us, " and assisted in defending this fortress against " the English." Major says, the Earl of Salisbury would have been taken, had he not been pulled back by some of his followers.

The two Earls, thus unsuccessful in their attempts, turned the siege into a blockade. The garrison, closely environed by sea and land, was reduced to great extremities, and must shortly have surrendered, had it not been relieved by the courage of Alexander Ramsay This * renowned hero, in the year 1338, when the English were masters of Edinburgh, concealed himself with a band of loyal men in the caves of Hawthornden, whence he issued forth, as occasion presented itself, and attacked small parties of the enemy and plundered their quarters. One of his excursions was to relieve Dunbar.

But let us pause a little and contemplate this fastness which Ramsay had chosen for his retreat. The situation of it is highly beautiful and interesting.

* J Major, ibid. —— Grose's Antiq of Scotland; Hawthornden Grose refers to Fordun, as his authority, probably Lib xiii I have not seen Fordun compleat

A lively river with a steep and lofty screen of rock on the one hand, and a wooded bank on the other, composes the ground-work of this admired scene. Grose has employed both his pencil and his pen to give us an idea of it. Hawthornden is a small fortress or castellated mansion, situated on a high projecting rock, overhanging the river North Esk, about two miles below Roslin Castle. Not far from Roslin Castle is Roslin Chapel, or the Chapel in the woods, that wonder of the masonic art, and opposite to it, somewhat lower down the stream, is a cavern almost inaccessible, where Ramsay probably posted some of his companions. The Caves where he fixed his own habitation, are situated still lower down the stream, underneath the present mansion of Hawthornden, with which they are connected by a deep draw-well. The entrance into them is in the side of a perpendicular rock of great height, above the river, to which you descend by twenty-seven high steps, cut in the rock; then passing along a board, about the length of five feet, and breadth of ten inches, you mount the rock on eight steps, and arrive at the mouth of the cave. On entering it you find caves cut in the rock on either hand, with pigeon holes to admit the light. That on the left hand is a long and narrow trance or passage, ascended to by two steps, of the length of seventy-five feet, and breadth of six, vulgarly called the King's gallery, near the upper end of which is a narrow dungeon, denominated the King's Bed-chamber. The range on the right side of these caverns, is much less than that which we have just described on the left It is hollowed out only to the length of twenty-one feet, and breadth of six feet, and is descended to by two steps. It is called the King's Guard Room. In descending the rock, before you pass the board, there is a grotto scooped out of the rock, of a modern workmanship, called the Cypress Grove, wherein, it is said, Drummond composed his poems, and conversed with his friend Ben Jonson, who walked from London to see him.

A variety of incredible and superstitious stories have been fabricated respecting the depth of these excavations, particularly of one formerly stiled the Elves-cave, the original entrance into which has been stopt by a fall of the rock,

Several delightful walks through the woods, on the sides of the rocks, are laid out with taste and judgement, seeming rather like the work of nature than of art, and benches of rude stone are judiciously deposited at some of the most striking points of view *.

Hawthornden itself with its ruined tower, crested with a sycamore tree, growing in its upper story, adds a characteristic feature to the deep and woody glen which it ennobles. It is the property of Bishop Abernethy Drummond.

These three caverns, by their amazing great strength in access, furnished a safe shelter for Ramsay and his companions. That brave Man

* This description is extracted from Grose's Antiquities, and Maitland's History of Edinburgh

was moved with † compassion, when he heard of the hardships to which the garrison of Dunbar was reduced. Accordingly, without suffering himself to be appalled by the danger of the enterprize, he embarked with forty resolute men, and a great quantity of provisions, and taking advantage of a dark, stormy night, eluded the vigilance of the Genoese gallies, stationed by the English to blockade the harbour, and landed safely at the Water-gate of the Castle. That night having joined a great part of the garrison to his own men, he sallied forth on the besiegers, who little expected

---

† J. Major, Lib. 5. c. 15.——Buchanan, Lib. 9 Rex 99 J. Major tells us, Lib. 1. c. 5. that when he was a Student at Cambridge, the Scholars carried bows and swords Perhaps it might be about the 33d year of Henry viiith, when an Act was past to encourage archery Had he been alive now he would have seen, not Scholars only, but the whole nation, starting up like the heroine of this poem, and harnessing for battle.

such an attack from a famished and exhausted garrison, and made a dreadful carnage of them. The following night he returned, unobserved, as he came. The two Earls soon afterwards raised the siege; being called away by Edward the Third to assist in his successes by sea and land over the French. With these he consoled himself for the little fruit of his Scottish expeditions.

That year, 1338, or as others say the year after, Ramsay made an excursion into England. He had often shewn his prowess in smaller matters, and with a few followers, he now resolved to undertake a larger enterprize. Ramsay far excelled the rest of his countrymen in military glory. Fathers sent their sons to him as the only master of the art of war. No man was reckoned a compleat soldier, who had not fought under his banners. The people therefore flocked to him at the *bridle* of Hawthornden (as Major calls it) where he had fixed his habitation. At length having collected a large army, he broke through the Scottish *border* or marches, and laid waste Northumberland. As he was returning, laden with spoil, the Northumbrians flew to arms, and drawing together a large body of forces from the different fortresses, they pursued him with confident hopes of success. Ramsay having disposed his infantry in ambush, and sent his plunder forward, instructed his horse to fly in apparent disorder on the approach of the Northumbrians, as if they were panic-struck, and to form themselves again by the sound of the trumpet, soon after they had past the place where their foot lay concealed. The Northumbrians fell into the snare. Seeing their enemies fly before them, they thought the victory their own, and pressed on also in disorder to cut them to pieces; when on the appointed signal, the Scots faced about, and gave them a reception they little expected. At the same time the infantry coming out of their lurking place, fell upon them in their rear, and put them entirely to the rout.

Thus did these brave and loyal Scots revenge themselves on their enemies, and exemplify the mottoes, *Nemo me impuné lacessit*, and *Noli me tangere*. Thus did they rid themselves of their invaders, and recover their country for David, their beloved Sovereign, then an exile in France, who soon afterwards came over to them to their great joy.

Whilst we admire the great qualities of Ramsay, we cannot but lament the disastrous times in which he lived, of which his sad catastrophe at Hawick is a proof. The kingdoms were not then happily united as they now are. The frontiers were subject to frequent inroads and perpetual alarms. Moss Troopers a sort of savage free-booters or banditti, carried on their trade of blood with impunity. Hereditary quarrels, called deadly feuds, were generated between families, and prosecuted with the most unexampled ferocity and tracts of country which are now covered with cultivation and the peaceful arts of husbandry, were then barren and desolate, the frightful abode of rapine, terror and death. One cannot read these accounts, without feeling a grateful sense for the blessings of the Union.

The Castle of Dunbar is boldly seated on two rocks projecting into the sea, and connected by a natural bridge of rock, consisting of *two arches*. One of these *gigantic arches* seems to have served as a * *porch* to the Water-gate. Through it may be seen the *Bass* rock or island, at the distance of a few miles, hanging very majestically over the sea. One of the rocks on which the Castle was built, jets out much further into the sea than the other, and in many places the water runs under it, through caverns formed by fissures in the stone. It contains also a large natural *cavern*, not incommoded with water, with *fissures* that serve for windows.

It is needless to observe that the Rose, Thistle, Shamrock and Lily, were severally borne on the

* Pennant's Tour into Scotland, Dunbar.

arms of England, Scotland, Ireland and France. The Shamrock is White Dutch Clover or Trefoil. The Harp also is a device belonging to Ireland: and the Liffey is a river which runs into the sea at Dublin.

Black Agnes,

or the

DEFENCE OF DUNBAR

BY AGNES, COUNTESS OF MARCH,

IN THE YEAR 1338

———————

§. 1.

" And do they come ?" *black* Agnes cry'd,

" Nor storm, nor midnight stops our toes ;—

" Well then, the battle's chance be try'd,

" The Thistle shall out-thorn the Rose."

She spake and started from her bed,

And cas'd her lovely limbs in mail;

The helmet on her *coal-black* head

Sluic'd o'er her eyes,—an iron veil!

In her fair hand she grasp'd a spear,

A baldrick o'er her shoulder flung;

While loud the bugle-note of war,

And Dunbar's *cavern'd echoes* rung.

Then to the castle-yard she sped,

Where her worn troops in order stood:

" Spare all you can, my friends," she said,

" Nor idly dip your dirks in blood.

" Select a band in dangers try'd,

" And guard the *rifted cavern* well."

Strait down it's hideous mouth they hied,

And heard the sea-storm's mingled yell,

Chamber'd in gloom.   On turrets high,

The dim wave sparkling far below,

The watchmen stretch the eager eye,

And anxious wait th' approaching foe

Dauntless, on wings of storm, the foe

Urges his course towards the cliff,

Then hoists the Scottish flag, and lo !

A friend——'tis Ramsay and relief !

On hinges harsh the Sea-gate turns,

The *giant-porch* with sullen roar

The restless waves ingulfs and spurns

Impatient Ramsay leaps ashore.

O'erjoy'd, the Countess scarce could speak,

But strait her beaver up she flung,

Survey'd and wip'd his sea-beat cheek,

And on his neck her broad sword hung

Then thus · " Whilst these *rock-arches* stand,

" Or yon huge Bass o'erhangs the sea,

" O Ramsay, may my native land

" Ne'er want a gallant Scot like Thee."

Ramsay reply'd · " At Hawthornden,

" Where chaunted vigils charm the night

" From Roslin's choirs, these fearless men

" Cradled, like birds, in the rock's height,

" The *Cave* their nest,—(there North Esk flows

" Midst castled woods,)—by night, by day,

" Harrass'd and watch'd and vex'd their foes,

" Like the gaunt wolf that prowls for prey.

" Hearing that Famine, pitiless,

" Consum'd thy men whom battle spar'd,

" These Forty, touch'd with thy distress,

" To serve Thee ev'ry danger dar'd.

" " Prowess," they said, " and engines fail—

" " But Want breaks down her castlesteads !

" " Come Ramsay bend the frozen sail,

" " And bear her all her valour needs."

" Fair Countess, thro' a stormy sea,

" Darkling, we pass'd yon hostile ships ;

" 'Tis well, for we are prais'd by Thee,

" And honour kindles at thy lips.

" A nation's love ! a nation's joy !

" Thy deeds on ev'ry tongue shall live,

" Thy smiles shall gladden ev'ry eye,

" Thy griefs *have* made a nation grieve.

" Soon shalt Thou weave the festive dance,

" And sing the song of peace again:

" The gath'ring cloud that bursts on France

" Shall clear our northern skies from rain.

" *Four* times has Edward's bugle-horn

" Been heard on Caledonian hills:

" Tir'd with his sport, with brambles torn,

" No more our woods with groans he fills.

" No more he'll sleep on Grampian snows,

" France will an easier quarry yield:

" There he may mould his Provence-Rose,

" And fix the Lilies on his shield. (A)

" The *deadly feud* (B) is now begun,

· The bloody gauntlet down is cast,

" Edward has claim'd the Salic crown .

" Long will that idle quarrel last.

" These ling'ring Earls (c) will soon depart,

" And Scotland from her wrongs be free :

" The King of ev'ry Scottish heart

" Shall owe his safe return to Thee."

So saying, with a soldier's pride,

The sword which late the Countess wore,

The guerdon rich that grac'd his side,

He drew and kiss'd,—then added more.

" Thine Earl, when David cheers the land,

" Shall win the royal Stranger's love:

" Thy sword, within my willing hand,

" THIS NIGHT thy beauty's power shall prove."

----

§. 2.

THAT NIGHT cost many mothers *dear*.—

Ramsay, no truant to his word,

Wrought England's grief:—their bed, their bier,—

Sleeping in death—they drench'd his sword.

THAT YEAR Northumbria saw with grief

Her plunder'd towns involv'd in smoke

No gallant knight brought *her* relief,

When Ramsay thro' the *border* broke. (D)

She arm'd.——In ambush Ramsay lay,

His horse in *seeming* fear retreat;

She *hurries* on to win the day——

She grasps *at* victory——in defeat.

Why, England, from a Bruce's brow

The *vengeful* Thistle wouldst thou tear?

Rather strike Crery's Lilies low.

Touch not the Thistle thou *shalt* wear. (E)

§. 3.

Those days of trouble now are past :

English and Scots, like Twins, agree :

No more their savage joy is—waste ;

And bloody fight their revelry.

No fierce Moss-Troopers (F) now combine

To riot o'er their neighbour's right .

No hamlets on the banks of Tyne (G)

In painful watches pass the night.

Once Howard (11) curb'd the guilty land,

And slept behind his iron door

Harness'd in terror, his command

The sternest form of justice wore.

Then deadly feuds and injur'd pride,

Goaded them on to deeds of blood.

They in the slaughter'd bullock's hide,

Their ready caldron, seeth'd their food. (1)

Hush'd is this fierce domestic war ·

In peace each tills his *little* farm :

No beacons blazing from afar,

And smoking villages, alarm.

Lord Percy might *his pleasure take* (K)

By Twiot and *the river Tweed*—

With hound and horn their echoes wake,

And not one gallant Briton bleed

---

§. 4

England! to form thy wreath of love,

Rose, Thistle, Shamrock freely blend—

—(Three realms in One, united move,

Can storms a three-fold cable rend?)— (L)

Sweet Shamrock brings her trefoil-braid

Her harp the triple union greets :

Who then shall make thy Sons afraid ?

Dare France invade thy peaceful seats ?

Ask him if Crecy be forgot,

Won by thy *single* chivalry ?

Tell him, the *never*-conquer'd Scot

And Liffey's Sons now fight by Thee

Tell him what *bulwarks* guard thy seas

Read him thy *muster-rolls at length*

Tell him—thy strength lies not in These—

But God alone is all thy strength.

Ah ! might thy negro-traffic cease !

May God, thy *scourge* and *guilt* remove !

Mourn o'er thy *guilt*—in *Him* seek peace—

His banner o'er thee shall be love. (M)

NOTES.

(A) THIS was the year, viz. 1338, in which Edward the Third unwisely quartered the arms of France with his own, and advanced his claim to that crown, contrary to the uniform custom of the realm and the spirit of the Salic law—the source of many bitter wars.

(B) A deadly feud is *properly* an hereditary quarrel between two families. Many caufes of these feuds existed before the union of England

and Scotland, and they were prosecuted with the most savage and unrelenting barbarity.

(c) The Earls of Salisbury and Arundel, whom Edward had left behind him to besiege Dunbar, were soon afterwards called home, together with their army, to attend him in his French expeditions

(d) In the year 1603, King James the First, in order to extinguish all memory of past hostilities between his kingdoms, prohibited the name of *borders* any longer to be ufed, substituting in its place that of *Middle Shires*, for the counties bordering on Scotland and England. Grose's Antiq. Berwick. Hence probably the phrase, *He comes out of the Shires*

(ᴋ) The second line of this stanza refers to the motto, *Nemo me impuné lacessit.* The last line refers to, *Noli me tangere.*

(ꜰ) Moss Troopers were a sort of banditti or free-booters that used to infest the *borders* by their destructive inroads, burning whole villages, and driving away cattle. For this they were liable to be called in question at the Courts held by the Lord Wardens of the Marches. Many Acts of Parliament were past to restrain them.

(ᴏ) Bishop Ridley, a native of Wilmonstwick in Tyne-dale, alludes to this subject very pathetically in a religious conference which he held with Bishop Latimer in prison, a little before their joint martyrdom.

Gilpin's Life of Latimer, §. X

(H) Lord William Howard, of Naworth Castle, in Cumberland, was the third son and second surviving son of Thomas, the unfortunate Duke of Norfolk, in the reign of Elizabeth, and the common Ancestor of the Earls of Carlisle and of the Howards of Corby. His bed-chamber, with its furniture and iron door, is still to be seen at Naworth There also are his dungeons. He is yet remembered in the traditions of the common people, and seems to have been well adapted to curb their lawless and turbulent spirit at the time in which he lived.

(I) See a striking passage from Froissard, in Hume's History, near the beginning of the reign of Edward the Third—a description of a Scottish army on its march.

(ᴋ) The popular ballad of Chevy Chace, to which this alludes, though not a true history, is nevertheless an exact picture of the manners of those unhappy times which preceded the union.

(ʟ) Ecclesiastes, ɪv. 12.

(ᴍ) Canticles, ɪɪ. 4

FINIS.

Printed by Bye and Law, St John's Square, Clerkenwell

Lightning Source UK Ltd.
Milton Keynes UK
UKHW021850190721
387437UK00003B/373

9 781375 036399